The NILE

The NILE

Geoffrey Moorhouse
Photography by Kazuyoshi Nomachi

BARRIE & JENKINS
LONDON

First published in 1989 by Barrie & Jenkins Limited,
289 Westbourne Grove, London W11 2QA

Photographs and captions © 1989 The Guidebook
Company Limited and Kazuyoshi Nomachi.
Introduction © 1989 The Guidebook Company
Limited and Geoffrey Moorhouse.

Designed by Joan Law Design & Photography

Colour separations and printing by Toppan Printing
Co. (H.K.) Ltd.

Endpaper maps — Cosmographia Tabvlae by Clavdii
Ptolemaei © 1978 Iwanami Shoten Publisher's, Tokyo.

British Library Cataloguing in Publication Data
Moorhouse, Geoffrey, *1931*–
  The Nile: a photographic odyssey.
  1. Africa. Nile River region. Description &
  travel
  I. Title
  916.2′0455

  ISBN 0-7126-3494-0

*Tisisat Falls. The Blue Nile drains from Lake Tana
on the Ethiopian Plateau and plunges down these falls
19 miles later. From this point the river flows in a
canyon until it reaches the desert of the Sudan to
merge with the White Nile at Khartoum.*

The White Nile

This Dinka tribesman inhabits a vast marshy area in southern Sudan known as the Sudd. Rising in Lake Victoria, the White Nile flows through this swamp in a northwesterly course, its progress impeded by the masses of vegetation growing in the basin. In this inhospitable land the cattle-breeding Dinka and Nuer tribes have endured the heat, humidity and ravages of mosquito-borne disease for thousands of years.

The Blue Nile

Christian worshippers in Lalibela gather around a church cut out of the ground. Lalibela is near the Tekeze River, a tributary of the Atbara River which flows into the Nile some 200 miles downriver from Khartoum. The devout orthodox Christians shown here share much of the cultural heritage of the people of Ethiopia's highlands where the Blue Nile has its source.

The Nile

Near the Atbara River in northern Sudan farmers cross a shallow stream on their way home. The Atbara, which like the Blue Nile also rises in Ethiopia, is the last tributary of the Nile. It flows into the mainstream 200 miles north of Khartoum. From here, the Nile passes through desert until it enters Egypt.

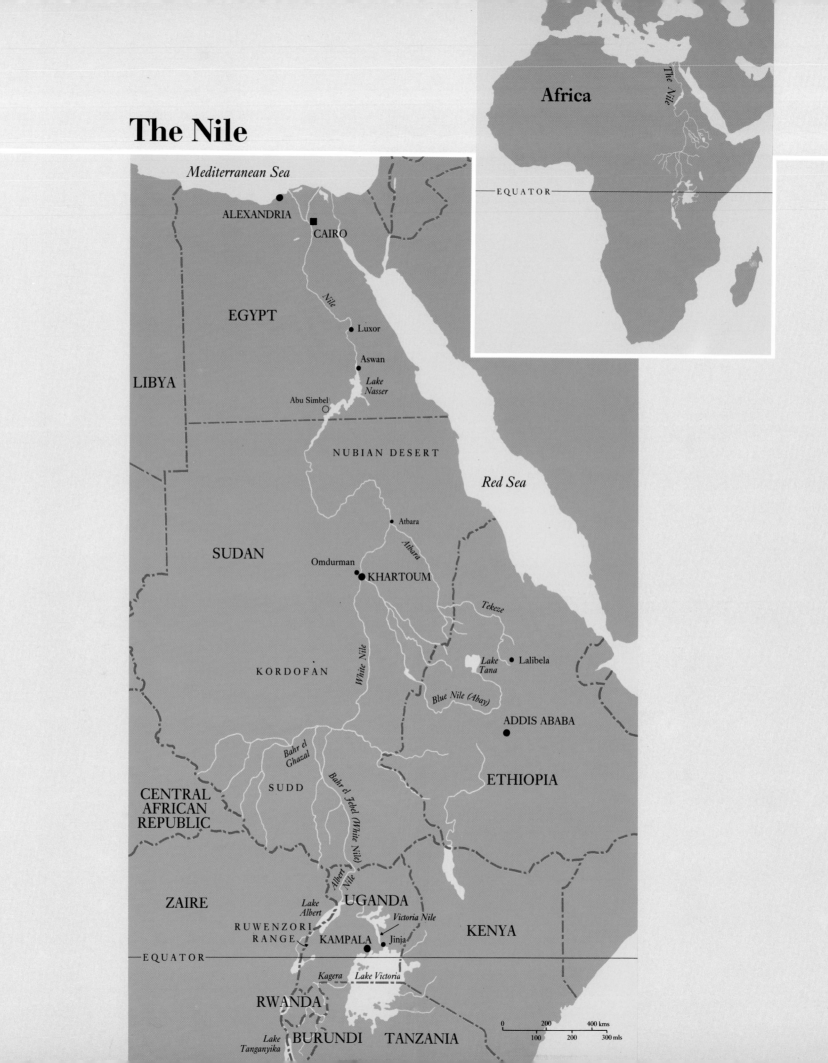

The Nile

Mediterranean Sea

ALEXANDRIA

■ CAIRO

EGYPT

Nile

● Luxor

Aswan ●

Lake Nasser

Abu Simbel ○

LIBYA

NUBIAN DESERT

Red Sea

Atbara ●

Atbara

SUDAN

Omdurman ●● KHARTOUM

Tekeze

KORDOFAN

White Nile

Lake Tana ● Lalibela

Blue Nile (Abay)

ADDIS ABABA ●

Bahr el Ghazal

SUDD

ETHIOPIA

CENTRAL AFRICAN REPUBLIC

Bahr el Jebel (White Nile)

Albert Nile

ZAIRE

Lake Albert

UGANDA

RUWENZORI RANGE

Victoria Nile

KAMPALA ● ● Jinja

KENYA

EQUATOR

Kagera *Lake Victoria*

RWANDA

BURUNDI   TANZANIA

Lake Tanganyika

0	200	400 kms
100	200	300 mls

Africa

The Nile

EQUATOR

Contents

Introduction

IT IS NOT LENGTH that distinguishes the Nile most considerably from all its great rivals. At 4160 miles from source to outfall, it *is* — only just ahead of the Amazon — the longest river in the world; but that statistic should be related to a couple of much more remarkable facts. In the first place, no other river traverses such a variety of landscapes, such a medley of cultures, such a spectrum of peoples as the Nile. And none has historically had such a profound material effect upon those who dwell along its banks, representing the difference between plenty and famine, between life and death, for multitudes since the beginning of time.

At the outset, of course, there are two River Niles, the Blue and the White. They join at Khartoum, almost in the middle of Sudan, and by then the first of them has already flowed a thousand miles from the east, where it issues from Lake Tana in the Ethiopian highlands, down a thundering waterfall. Its origins lie in a wild and rugged land, whose warrior people can trace their history back to Solomon and the Queen of Sheba. Their son Menelik became the first emperor in a line that was to stretch unbroken until quite recently. Although the mosque has long been as common a sight as the church along these early stages of the Blue Nile, Ethiopia from the fourth century onwards was unique in Africa, in effect a Christian theocracy, its rulers — until the Emperor Haile Selassie was deposed by communists in 1974 — devout members of the Coptic Church which had spread from Egypt, where it flourishes still.

The White Nile, meanwhile, has travelled almost twice as far before reaching the confluence at Khartoum. Its life starts in spring water pouring down a gully in Burundi, one of the tiniest nations in the world, where the local Tutsi tribe know it as Kasumo — the gusher. This is four degrees south of the Equator, deep in the Africa of tropical growth and predatory beasts, south of the Ruwenzori, the legendary Mountains of the Moon, where the gorilla is supremely at home in all but impenetrable forest. With over 4000 miles to go before the Mediterranean is attained, a small pyramid has been erected on a rocky hill above the source, with a bronze plaque on which are the words *Caput Nili*. This is the work of the German explorer Burkhart Waldecker, who in 1937 at last ended man's long quest to determine the true origins of the almighty Nile. Until then it had been assumed that we need look no further south than Lake Victoria, ever since the Englishman John Speke traced the river to that inland sea in 1862. But Waldecker remained unsatisfied until he had found the main feeder of the lake half way down its western shore, and doggedly followed it back to that potent source.

Relief from the Temple of Hatshepsut at Luxor (ca 1498–1483 BC), on the west bank of the Nile.

From Burundi the White Nile rushes into the neighbouring states of Tanzania and Rwanda before entering Lake Victoria. It then continues across Uganda, flirts briefly with Lake Albert and, by now a great waterway 1000 miles from its source, reaches Sudan. So far, it has flowed through lush vegetation, areas of high rainfall, where game is plentiful and where the riparian tribes herd their cattle and grow crops of maize and beans, sorghum and cassava. Theirs is a primitive existence, but it is not as desolate as life can be for some who live further to the north on the Nile's course.

Before long this becomes indistinct as it encounters the Sudd, which is Arabic for 'obstacle', and which in reality is a swamp as big as England. Enormous platforms of papyrus and water hyacinth grow out of the primeval ooze, forming a wilderness in which human beings and even quite large boats have been hopelessly, fatally lost. The solitary steamer that in recent years has conveyed passengers and cargo the 900 miles between Juba and Kosti has done so laboriously, taking a week to travel downstream and 12 or more days to go the other way, only after the crew have hacked a passage through the dense stalks and branches choking the channel.

For a decade or more an attempt was begun to bypass this Sudd by cutting the Jonglei Canal from one bend in the White Nile to another 224 miles away. The object has been to improve the vigour of the river by avoiding the swamp, where it loses half its volume in evaporation; also to regulate the rise and fall of the waters on which the fate of millions lower down the Nile still depends. When the canal is finished, it will signal the beginning of the end of the Sudd, its gradual drainage, which in turn means that there should be a dramatic fall in the local rate of malaria and other diseases that thrive upon tracts of stagnant water. But work on the canal came to a standstill in 1982, with a third of the way still to go, as a result of the civil war in the southern Sudan.

Just before Khartoum, equatorial Africa is left behind, and desert begins. By the time the Blue and White Niles merge there, each is in a different world from the one it has so far known. The landscape changes from every conceivable, every delicately different shade of green, to an equally subtle palette of colours which are harshly bleached by the glare of daylight and can only be appreciated in their full range, from purple to cream, as the sun is beginning to go down the sky. Normally a cooling breeze from the rivers soothes the Sudanese capital in the scorching heat; but the frightening power of the Niles became apparent in 1988, when their floodwaters devastated the city and its twin community of Omdurman. Life hereabouts — and all the way to Egypt — is precarious for the inhabitants at every season of any year. The desert is devoid of any romance for those who must abide in it.

Black Africa has not yet been abandoned, though, and in Khartoum's great marketplace one may see perhaps the most remarkable mingling of races in the whole continent. Here are various degrees of negritude in the persons of Dinka, Shilluk and Nuer, whose heads and torsos are marked with elaborate cicatrices painfully incised at puberty. Here are much stockier people from northern Sudan, with skins that were paled by generations of coupling with Arabs; the Beja from close to the border with Egypt; and the Nubians, who served the ancient pharaohs as soldiers, artisans and intermediaries with Black Africa. Then there are the pure Arabs, who were responsible for bringing Islam to this part of the world.

There is no getting away from Islam here. At the presidential palace beside the Blue Nile in Khartoum are the steps on which General Charles Gordon met his death in 1885 at the hands of a mob following the Muslim prophet, the Mahdi. Across the White Nile from the capital, in Omdurman, is the Mahdi's tomb, with a crescent and the point of a spear topping its silver dome. The Mahdi had led his dervishes against the British in *jihad*, a holy war, and although his army was decimated in a terrible retribution for Gordon's death, at the Battle of Omdurman 13 years later, the dervishes were not extinguished. Indeed, they are responsible for one of the most memorable moments any traveller along the Nile will ever know.

Before sunset each Friday they gather outside an Omdurman mosque, scores of them forming into a circle. Drummers beat time while the dervishes shuffle round under the leadership of an old man who is said to be the Mahdi's grandson. Gradually the pace quickens, excitement mounts, spectators begin to ululate. Suddenly one of the cloaked figures in the circle breaks away and starts spinning on one leg, flourishing a whip to help his balance, while his green and orange cloak swirls through the air. Soon the ground is full of wildly spinning figures, the drumming goes berserk, and men begin to spin to the ground in dizziness as the performance reaches its crescendo, which it achieves about an hour after the performance has begun. It stops only when the sun disappears below the horizon behind the mosque. Quite abruptly there is silence, lassitude, where there had been almost unendurable gyration and noise. What the bystander has witnessed is a ballet of the most athletic kind: but most of all he has seen a rare religious fervour.

The Niles, united at last, flow majestically to the north, the surrounding desert relieved only by thin strips of cultivation along the riverside for some distance beyond Khartoum. Sixty miles downstream is the Sixth Cataract, where the river plunges between high walls and around huge boulders that make it impossible for navigation. Four more of these obstacles appear before Egypt is reached; also Lake Nasser, 300 miles long and artificially created in 1963, at the building of the Aswan High Dam.

The dam was constructed to solve that age-old problem of Egypt, which still bedevils Sudan: how to prevent an entire nation from being at the mercy of this river. Before it was built, there were years of drought in Egypt, when not enough water came down from the highlands of Central Africa; or there were years of flood, when just as many people and animals perished in a different fashion. And although some scientists claim that a number of unforeseen side-effects are less than welcome — a reduction of fish stocks in the delta, for example — it is generally agreed that the Aswan Dam, and the controlled expanse of water in Lake Nasser behind it, have been a tremendous success. Vast areas of Egypt have been steadily irrigated, giving two or even three crops a year instead of only one at the best of times. Large areas of desert have been reclaimed. Hydroelectricity has led to new industries in Upper Egypt.

There was a cost, however, and it was paid by the Nubians, whose ancestral lands lay where the lake now slops and swells. Some 90,000 of them were forced to uproot and move elsewhere in both Egypt and Sudan. The steamer that takes a couple of days to sail from Wadi Halfa down to Aswan is cruising over the drowned folk memories of an entire race, as well as the submerged ruins of their former prosperity. From the steamer's decks it is possible to see abandoned dwellings gradually disintegrating on the barren hillsides just above the shoreline. You can also glimpse the temples of Abu Simbel, built 3200 years ago to the glory of Ramesses II, and moved 212 feet higher up their hillside to avoid the inundation of 1963, in the biggest archaeological salvage operation of all time.

Below the dam is the First Cataract; and below that the evidence of ancient civilisation is apparent almost every mile. At Elephantine Island, much patronised by tourists who have come up the river in luxury steamships, it is possible to see the stone nilometer, engraved with marks by which the pharaoh's officials related the river's seasonal rise to local taxation. After a while, temples appear: Kom Ombo, which is dedicated to the falcon-headed Horus and to Sobek, the crocodile god; Edfu, also to Horus, and the best preserved temple in the country, virtually in the same condition its builders left it in a few hundred years before Christ. At Luxor, there is more antiquity than most of us would wish to contemplate in a week, with the haunting tumbledown epic of masonry on the east bank at Karnak, and the pharaonic tombs that sprawl extensively across the Valley of the Kings on the other side of the river.

The Nile is a fully working waterway now, as it never has been before except for a few miles around Khartoum. As well as the floating hotels that bring sophistication and wealth from all corners of the earth, there are humbler but more graceful craft, wide-beamed feluccas with two masts and lateens, which the boatmen propel with heavy oars when no wind stirs the sails (this tends to come from the north in winter, from the south in summer, but often the air along the Nile's middle stretches is inert). The country boats carry bricks, cement, grain, hay, earthenware pots, almost anything. As they travel downstream towards Cairo they have to look lively, for there they are joined by diesel-engined craft with blaring horns and attendant barges, which expect everyone else to get out of their way. In the wake of their engines, furrows of water go sloshing along the river's bank, where men irrigate their land by means of the ancient waterwheel they call *saqiya*.

The feluccas on the Nile give Cairo a touch of grace, which Africa's largest city otherwise all too often lacks, mixing humdrum modernity with demented traffic and some of the most awful shantytowns in creation. And shortly after shaking off this metropolis, the river begins to dissipate itself as it never did before. Hundreds of small canals and watercourses network the farmlands between Cairo and the sea, drawing their sustenance from the Nile and resulting in some of the most intensive cultivation of vegetables anywhere: cabbages and cauliflowers grow so big that the farmers carry them over their shoulders individually by the stalk, instead of under their arms.

The river thus reaches the Mediterranean through innumerable outlets, as well as through two well-marked channels which emerge at Dumyat and Rosetta, towns whose only distinction is that the Nile at last relinquishes Africa through them. This is, on the whole, a very discreet ending for the river after such a colossal journey. But a part of it flows into the sea through Alexandria, that port which in some ways feels more like the South of France than the Egyptian delta. Here Cleopatra killed herself, and here Alexander the Great's remains almost certainly lie in some unmarked spot. The Nile in Alexandria is thus touched with the sense of mystery and power that has attracted all mankind to the river since earliest times. It was these attributes that caused the Greek Herodotus to investigate as far as the First Cataract, 460 years before Christ was born. They impelled the Roman Emperor Nero to send an expedition much farther, until his legionairies were forced to turn back on meeting the fearful Sudd. They were responsible for the successive explorations of such 19th-century Westerners as Livingstone, Stanley, Baker, Burton and Speke, all of whom spent much of themselves in trying to find the source.

I know of no photographs which have captured the elements of the Nile as brilliantly as these of Kazuyoshi Nomachi. See the photographs of the Omdurman dervishes on pages 126–7, and look at the expressions on the faces of the two most prominent dancers. They have probably been gyrating for up to half an hour and they are beyond frenzy, out of control, utterly lost in some sensational ultimate of their faith. They have reached ecstacy, that most private of human conditions, even when, as here, it is a climax of public performance. Whether Nomachi is concentrating on landscape or people, he has succeeded in conveying images, telling circumstances, in a way that almost renders words superfluous. On page 44 he shows a Nuer boy shampooing his hair while a cow urinates over his head; and next to it is the picture of a lad performing cunnilingus on another beast so that, sexually stimulated, she will release more milk to feed him and his family. Those two photographs show exactly what is meant when we refer to a primitive society. To define the primitive, a writer would feel the need to tread delicately, so as not to seem superior, not to be passing judgement on someone who is no less worthy than himself. In doing so, he would probably obscure something of the reality he was trying to convey. Nomachi's artistry cuts through humbug, offers no apologies, says simply and starkly and *carefully* — Look, these are the ways that people here make the best of things.

Geoffrey Moorhouse
September 1988

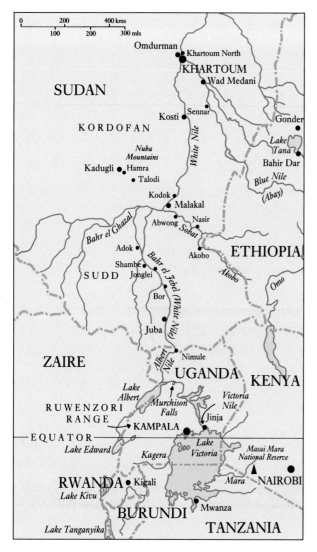

The White Nile

FROM THE HEART OF Central Africa comes a trickle that tumbles and swells quickly with rainwater and many mountain tributaries. This is the White Nile in its infancy, still hundreds of miles from Lake Victoria, that vast, freshwater sea once considered the source of the mighty river. The ascribed name 'Nile' appears on maps only after the point of efflux on the lake's north shore. From here to Lake Albert it is called the Victoria Nile, and along this stretch occurs a singular event, the river's dramatic 140-foot drop over Murchison Falls. Later, for 100 miles it is known as the Albert Nile before reaching the border of Uganda and the Sudan; thereafter local people call the majestic flow Bahr el Jebel, Sea of the Mountains. A last major geographical interruption of the White Nile is the awesome, unyielding Sudd, largest swamp in the world. After losing half its volume to evaporation within this languid morass, the river finally breaks free and carries northward to Khartoum, where it loses its identity by merging with the Blue Nile. Here at the confluence the derivation of the river's names becomes clear. The 'whiteness' of the White Nile, in fact a greyish-brown colour, contrasts with the dull green of the waters that have been given the generous and poetic appellation 'Blue Nile'.

A Nuba wrestler has covered himself with the ash of a burned acacia. The ash is considered holy. Male strength is prized by the Nuba, who regularly put it to the test in wrestling matches held as part of the December harvest festival.

The Ruwenzori mountain range on the border of Zaire and Uganda. A Greek merchant first named the range 'Mountains of the Moon'. The second-century geographer Ptolemy used this information to draw his world map; inaccurately he placed the source of the Nile in these mountains.

Right: *Waters from the Ruwenzori mountains rush down 8000 feet to the river below; here porters inch their way on slippery rocks in treacherous water.*

Bakonjo porters wading barefoot through the swamps
— covered with ice at higher altitudes — that
punctuate the mountain paths. Bakonjo tribespeople
were originally mountain hunters.

Left: *In the Ruwenzori mountains, one of the wettest
ranges in the world, Senecio forest flourishes at an
altitude of 12,500 to 15,500 feet, right up to the
glacier. The name 'Senecio' derives from the Latin and
refers to the hoary appearance of the leaves.*

Above left: *Elephants, Masai Mara National Reserve, Kenya.* Above right: *Egret, Murchison Falls National Park, Uganda.* Below: *Thomson's gazelle, Masai Mara.* Right: *Sunset at Masai Mara. The Mara River, which crosses the reserve, leads eventually to Lake Victoria.*

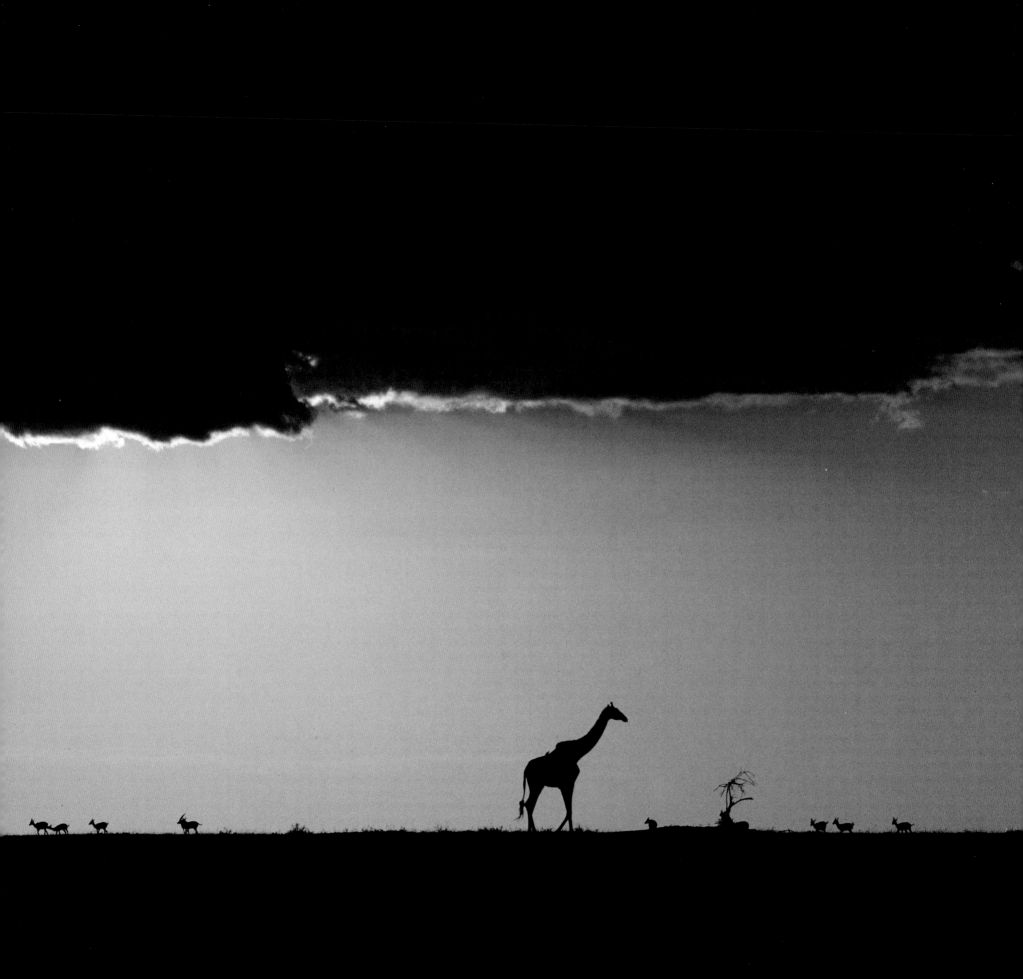

Young women of the Surma tribe in animal skins.

Left: *Once inhabitants along a mountainous tributary to the White Nile, the Surma tribespeople now live on the Omo River in southern Ethiopia. Surma women cut the lower lip to insert ever increasing sizes of lip saucers — a custom which, it is thought, prevented them from being taken as slaves and so protected the whole tribe. The lip discs thus symbolize beauty for the Surma people.*

The White Nile — also known as the Victoria Nile because it issues from Lake Victoria — runs 125 miles before reaching Murchison Falls. Below the 140-foot falls, the river's flow becomes gentle and along this stretch crocodiles and hippopotamuses are found.

A hippopotamus in the Victoria Nile, below Murchison Falls.

Swamps near Shambe, in the vast marshy area of
papyrus and water plants known as the Sudd, or
'obstacle' in Arabic. Beginning a hundred miles from
Juba in southern Sudan and extending for some 430
miles to Malakal, the Sudd is a maze of thick
vegetation in which many explorers have lost
themselves. The White Nile runs a zigzag course
through it.

During the dry season, young men of the cattle-
breeding Dinka tribe take their herds to the lowland
and set up camps such as this one, with papyrus huts
and piles of smouldering cattle dung to repel insects.
When the rains come and the river waters are at their
highest, this land turns to marsh, compelling the
herders to abandon camp and to go to their village on
a hill.

A boy carries the head of a gazelle caught by his dog.

Left: *Men of the Dinka tribe, which numbers some 800,000, like the Nuer and Shilluk tribesmen, are remarkable for their slimness and height. Dinka men are the tallest, averaging almost six feet two inches.*

In the morning, after the cattle have been taken out, herdsmen collect their dung to dry in the sun. Cattle dung is important to the inhabitants of the Sudd, where malaria is endemic. The half-dried dung will be burned at night to keep away disease-carrying mosquitos and other insects.

Right: Sunset over a Dinka camp. A tribesman lights a small cow-dung fire; cattle returning from the day's grazing will be staked for the night. It is near the end of the dry season, and once the rains begin this area will be inundated.

An evening meal is prepared at twilight in this Nuer camp near Nasir.

Left: *Diminishing light at the end of day and smoke from fires give this scene a surreal quality. In the harsh environment, cattle cannot live without their human protectors; in turn, the smoke from cattle dung protects the tribespeople from malarial mosquitos.*

A young Dinka boy grooms his hair with ash, used as a deterrent to mosquitos and often smeared on the face and body as decoration.

Dinka men rest in a camp near Jonglei. These camps are chiefly occupied by young men; women and older people live in a village on a hill not far from the camp.

Following page: *At this Nuer camp near Nasir, cattle are milked and bled for food. The bleeding of cattle is common in East African societies, like this one, whose members rarely eat meat. The tribe's wealth is in its cattle, and there are many legends about how the animals were gifts of the gods to humans.*

A Nuer boy washes his hair in cow's urine. Because of the scarcity of water and proximity to their animals, these people have no concept of bodily waste as dirt; urine, like cattle dung, is a resource for survival.

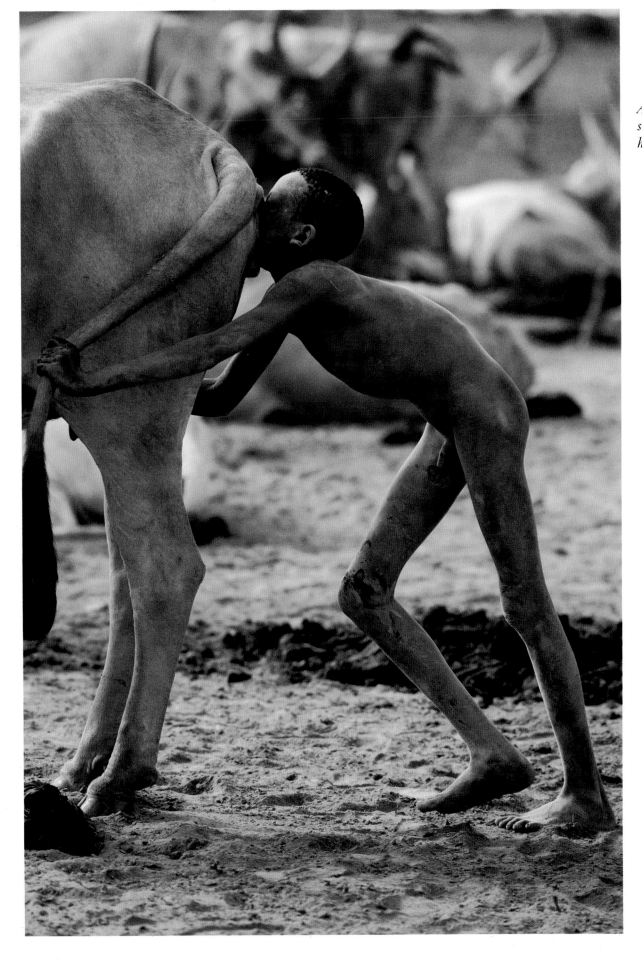

A Dinka boy sexually stimulates a cow to make her produce more milk.

Near Nasir, a Nuer boy sucks milk directly from the cow's udder; this is his only source of food for the morning.

The hollow calabash is used instead of a milk pail. In this Nuer tribe, milking is done chiefly by women and children. The milk is drunk or made into yoghurt for preserving food. Here a Nuer girl uses the cow's tail to wipe off spilled food.

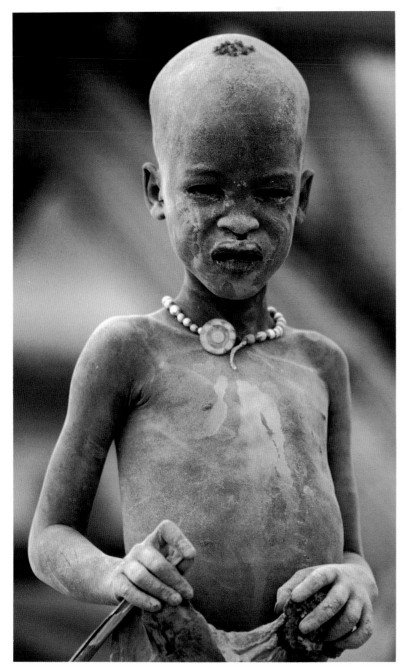

Daily rituals among the cattle-breeding tribes. Above and across: *a child just awake after a night asleep in the ash; a cow found dead is brought back for food; ceremonial tools — the scrotum of a goat filled with ash, and other animal parts — are part of Nuer worship; an old Dinka man; hair being groomed with an acacia thorn.*
Bottom across: *devotion to cattle is shown by polishing the horns; a Dinka man makes cattle rope from papyrus; hair-grooming.*

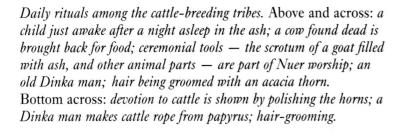

Dinka people dance in celebration of their cattle at each full moon.

Dinka dancing is simple but superbly balanced, often mimicking the exaltation of the sexual act.

Near Malakal, cattle-breeders have set this field afire,
just before the rainy season, to spur new growth.

For Dinka fishermen, who live in nest-like constructions in the marsh water, existence is less secure than that of the cattle-breeders on dry land.

A Dinka fisherman on a Sudd waterway near Shambe. Behind, the enormous floating tiers of water plants and papyrus, which often block the waterways, look as substantial as land.

The young Dinka people often wear corsets of beads, the colours varying with the age of the wearer.

These unstable canoes, scooped from logs, provide a ferry service for the Shilluk tribespeople between their dwelling place on the west bank of the White Nile to Malakal on the east bank. No bridge spans the river from Juba to Kosti, a distance of some 750 miles.

Following page: *A fisherman pulls his canoe forwards through a maze of floating plants and reeds along a Sudd waterway near Jonglei. He will cast a net in the evening and take it in by morning; the catch is likely to be Nile perch measuring over two feet long.*

Crocodiles and hippopotamuses are the greatest enemy of the Sudd fishermen; this man has lost his lower leg to a crocodile.

A crocodile below Murchison Falls. The ancient Egyptians revered the crocodile god Sobek, and the creatures were found in the Nile right up to the end of the 19th century. Sport hunting and the building of the first Aswan dam effectively prevented them from returning to Egypt, although they are now found in Lake Nasser.

A huge flock of birds might easily be mistaken for fast-moving black clouds as it sweeps along the bank of the Sobat River.

A Nuer boy plays in the Sobat River near Abwong.

Nuba girls dance to honour the winner of a wrestling match, near Kadugli.

Left: *A swarm of locusts in the acacia forest near Nuba Mountain. Accounts of crop-destroying locusts in Egypt go back to Biblical times.*

The colour of the desert rose is a startling contrast to the earthen tones of this small Nuba village near Talodi.

Right: *Wrestlers of the Nuba tribe rest under a giant baobab tree near Hamra. Although the tribe numbers less than 500,000, fifty different languages are spoken by the Nuba. It is said that they originated in several regions around the Nile but found refuge among the Nuba Mountains when fleeing from slave merchants.*

In the dry season these Nuba girls are forced to walk far to find water; then it must be carried halfway up the mountain to their village.

The Nuba house comprises four or five round huts surrounding a yard. This hut is used as a kitchen; the entrance is small and high to keep out cattle and rats.

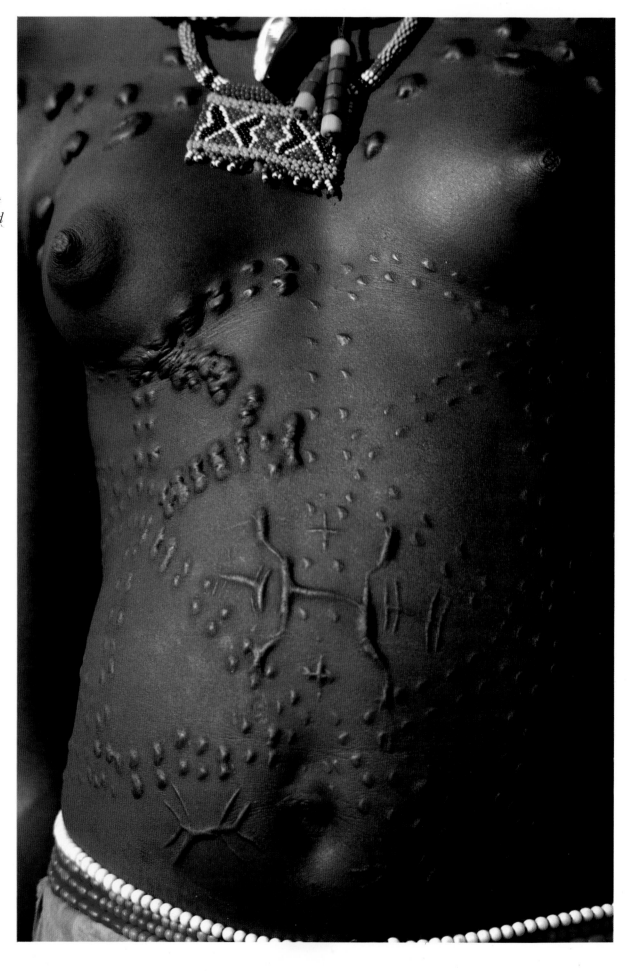

A sharp bamboo knife is used to make these cicatrice decorations, common to tribal African people. For a girl, the decorations are made first at the onset of menses and later at the birth of each new child.

Nuba women braiding hair.

Top left: *wrestlers enter an arena set in a wild field.*
Top right: *the winner is carried aloft; later he will be blessed by the villagers and dance for them.*
Bottom left: *a match in progress; it will be decided when one of the fighters falls.* Bottom right: *the winner, covered with the ashes of victory, will return to the ring to fight again.*

Sunset in the Nuba hills.

Twilight on the savannah.

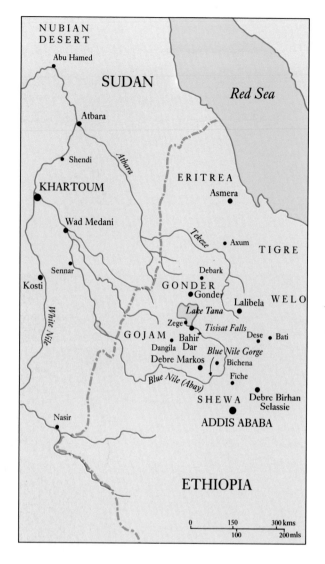

The Blue Nile

THE BLUE NILE, much shorter than the parent White Nile and never considered the true source, contributes an astonishing majority of the river's total volume. Its origin is the gentle overflow from Lake Tana, a serene lake 6000 feet high on the Ethiopian Plateau. Suddenly the tranquillity of this easy beginning is broken by the endless cannonade of Tisisat Falls. This marks the start of a gorge like none other on earth, a massive, long gash that cuts through the highlands in a huge bend, created by 400 miles of roiling, tumultuous water. In some places the walls of the gorge rise nearly 5000 feet from the river, enclosing a weird, difficult and beautiful environment where few humans live. The Blue Nile drops rapidly and only near the Sudan border does it slow down, becoming wide and warm. Eventually it enters the desert proper and travels northwestward for its rendezvous with the White Nile at Khartoum. This wild river links the extremely different, irreconcilable worlds of the mountain Ethiopians and the Arabs of desert and plain.

A famine refugee in Lalibela, holy place for orthodox Christan Ethiopians and a gathering place for the famine-stricken during the terrible drought of 1984—1985. In that drought, six million Ethiopians suffered severely and over a million died of starvation.

At the bottom of the falls. 'Tisisat' means smoking water in Ethiopian.

Left: *An aerial view of Tisisat Falls in October, just after the rainy season. At the end of the dry season in June, the falls will be virtually dry.*

The Blue Nile running through the highland valley. In the distance it is just possible to make out the only bridge that crosses the Blue Nile gorge.

Left: The highlands of Ethiopia are also known as Abyssinia. This verdant land provides rich harvests as long as there is rain.

The light, naturally buoyant paper-reed or papyrus boat is a standard means of transportation for the people of Lake Tana. Here oarsmen make the eight-hour journey to Bahir Dar to sell firewood.

Right: *This Old Kingdom tomb relief at Saqqara, Egypt, depicting a paper-reed boat, dates back to 2000 BC.*

Gonder Province women carry precious firewood in the rain. The Ethiopian forest has been stripped for firewood and no natural forest remains except eucalyptus.

Right: *Rain, though essential for life, can bring disastrous floods. Umbrellas and plastic covering offered little protection during this rainstorm in Addis Ababa in 1984. Ironically, most of Ethiopia had no rainfall in 1984—1985 and the ensuing famine took a terrible toll.*

*This field near Dangila in Gojam Province, Ethiopia,
shown just after the rainy season, will yield a good
harvest in December. That same year, Welo Province,
only 160 miles away, was afflicted by a prolonged
drought which took many lives.*

*Near Debre Markos, two sisters carry cattle dung
which will be used for fuel. It is February, during the
dry season.*

An Amhara girl in Lalibela. Amharas, most of whom are Christians, live in the Ethiopian highlands, and make up only a quarter of the Ethiopian population.

*The stone dwellings and lifestyle of the Christian
Ethiopians, whose holy place is Lalibela in Lasta
Province, have changed little since medieval times.*

The weekly market at Lalibela, where traders gather to sell clothing, herbal medicines and even rock salt from the Danakil Desert.

Right: In the village of Debark, in Gonder Province, an Islamic farmer has come to market.

Muslims pray over the body of a young famine victim at Bati in Welo Province. In late 1984, famine claimed 50–60 lives a day here and grave diggers worked without rest.

A young Amhara wife in Lalibela grieves for her husband. Both men and women express their grief openly, some scratching their cheeks until they bleed.

Left: *A funeral cortège of the Oromo tribe near Fiche.*

Following page: *Priests dance at the inner court of Bet Maryam (Church of St Mary), carved out of the rock. On 7 January Christian pilgrims from all over Ethiopia come to celebrate Christmas at Lalibela. Some walk for more than a week through the mountains to attend the festival.*

A painting of the Resurrection on the wall of the 15th-century Kebran Gabriel on a small island in Lake Tana. About 20 monasteries on the lake islands date back to the 12th century. They are all still kept up by monks.

Left: *Christmas: a monk preaches to pilgrims on Mount Tabor, one of many places of Biblical fame in Lalibela.*

*Pilgrims assemble at Lalibela during the week leading
up to Christmas. They camp in a field near the church
and pray morning and evening, their prayers
resounding on the walls along with the church bell.*

A Christian pilgrim, with a cross marked in holy ash on his forehead, at Lalibela.

The 'Fountain of Fecundity' at Bet Maryam in Lalibela. It is believed that women can conceive by bathing here at Christmas. Women take turns to jump in, guided by a safety rope.

A woman who cannot swim is hauled to safety after risking her life for the experience of the holy fountain.

*Medieval angels guard the door of a church in the
forest of Zege opposite Bahir Dar on Lake Tana.*

A Tabot, representing the Ark of the Covenant, contains a tablet inscribed with the Ten Commandments. It is wrapped in brocade and taken out of Bet Giorgis (Church of St George) at Lalibela for such festivals as the Timket (Epiphany). At its appearance worshippers bow in reverence.

Following page: *Priests at prayer in the cave of Bet Giorgis. These devotions precede the two-hour Tabot procession. The prayers are spoken in Geez, the original language of the Amhara, so it is unintelligible to the Ethiopians.*

Above: *Wearing a crown for the Timket.* Top right: *Deacons carrying a cross, leading the Tabot from Bet Giorgis (St George, shown in a painting behind).* Bottom right: *Tabot-carrying procession.*

Far left: *Angels painted on the church ceiling at Debre Birhan Selassie, Gonder Province.* Top left: *Paradise lost depicted on the wall of Kebran Gabriel monastery on an island in Lake Tana.* Bottom left: *Girls dance in front of the Tabot at the Timket Festival in Addis Ababa.*

117

At the climax of Timket, symbolizing the baptism of Christ, worshippers vie to splash themselves with consecrated water. Later each Tabot will be returned to its church in a procession of dancing and singing.

A worshipper in the early morning.

The Blue Nile in the dry season in the Ethiopian highlands, a rugged territory whose inhabitants live virtually beyond the reach of government administration. Attempts at a definitive survey of this stretch of the river continue; some outside surveyors have drowned or been shot.

*The Blue Nile running through the Sudanese desert,
where it provides the only source of water in a terrain
afflicted by heat, wind and sandstorms.*

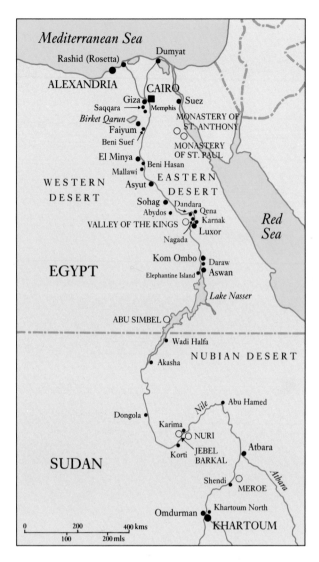

Map showing the Nile from the Mediterranean Sea through Egypt and Sudan to Khartoum. Labelled places include: Mediterranean Sea, Rashid (Rosetta), Dumyat, ALEXANDRIA, CAIRO, Giza, Suez, Saqqara, Memphis, Birket Qarun, MONASTERY OF ST. ANTHONY, Faiyum, Beni Suef, MONASTERY OF ST. PAUL, El Minya, Beni Hasan, Mallawi, EASTERN DESERT, WESTERN DESERT, Asyut, Sohag, Dandara, Abydos, Qena, Karnak, VALLEY OF THE KINGS, Luxor, Red Sea, Nagada, Kom Ombo, Daraw, Elephantine Island, Aswan, EGYPT, Lake Nasser, ABU SIMBEL, Wadi Halfa, NUBIAN DESERT, Akasha, Abu Hamed, Dongola, Nile, Karima, NURI, JEBEL BARKAL, Korti, Atbara, SUDAN, Shendi, MEROE, Atbara, Omdurman, Khartoum North, KHARTOUM. Scale: 0 200 400 kms; 100 200 mls.

The Nile

SOUTH OF KHARTOUM the Nile in its dual form certainly is 'a complicated stream'. To the north, however, the geography of the river becomes starkly simple. A ribbon of brown water wends its way through terrible deserts, and with the exception of one final tributary, the Atbara, no contributing rivers and virtually no rainfall nourish the Nile. In northern Sudan and Egypt the river is the only hope of life; waters that irrigate the green banks today come from the same sources that allowed ancient Nubia and the civilization of the pharaohs to flourish. Beyond the Aswan Dam and its great artificial lake, the Nile proceeds through the heart of Egypt, past temples, pyramids and ruins, past fields of wheat and vegetables, on to the capital of Cairo. At last the torpid, silt-rich river expends itself in the Nile Delta, Egypt's cornucopia. Only two main branches reach the Mediterranean Sea, final resting place for a river that began half a continent away.

Ramesses II ruled for 67 years (ca 1279–1212 BC); this head from a fallen statue of the king is at his temple, the Ramesseum, at Thebes (Luxor) on the west bank of the Nile.

Following spread: *Date palms line the Atbara River, also known as the 'Black Nile'. Here, in the dry season, a farmer crosses the shallow water with his donkey.*

Left, right and above: *At a mosque outside the city of Omdurman opposite Khartoum, sufis, or Islamic mystics, gather to praise Allah in feverish prayer and dance.*

A two-year-old girl is carried to her grave in the small village of Korti on the Nile. After the burial, the men pour Nile water over her tomb.

Top and bottom left: *Female villagers, not allowed to attend the burial ceremony, call to express their condolences.* Above: *The mother and family of the dead child; the father was working in Khartoum at the time, and did not hear the news until several days after the funeral.*

Left: *The irrigated fields along the river from Khartoum to Atbara yield rich crops. This farmer at the village of Dongola inspects the coming harvest of sorghum.*

A fruit market at Shendi in northern Sudan.

A schoolroom at Akasha on Lake Nasser. When asked about their future occupations, the boys said they wanted to be drivers or doctors, the girls nurses.

Schoolteachers at Akasha.

Left: *A T-shaped cicatrice on the face of a nomadic woman shows she is from the Jaliyin tribe of northern Sudan. In southern Sudan, cuts are made on the forehead instead.*

There is no bridge across the Nile for the nearly 1200 miles between Khartoum and Aswan, so sailing boats and engine-powered ferries are essential transport. Here an Arab man wrestles to get his donkey onto a boat near Dongola.

Nomads bringing their cattle to the river near Omdurman.

At a small village near Atbara women come to the Nile for water. Their brightly coloured cloth tobes is typical north Sudanese dress.

Near Shendi, a young nomad of the Jaliyin tribe that keeps camels and goats.

Left: *Jebel Barkal, near the site of ancient Napata, rises sheer from the desert. Here the Nile has come from the northeast through barren and largely uninhabited land. These pyramids, built for the early rulers of the kingdom of Kush (ninth to fourth century BC) are smaller and more steeply angled than those of the Egyptian Pharaohs of the Old Kingdom.*

A camel caravan heading north from Abu Hamed to Wadi Halfa in the Nubian Desert. After resting in Wadi Halfa, the camels will be taken north to the Aswan cattle market to be sold for meat.

Nubian women in traditional black dress travelling by felucca on the river at Aswan. After the completion of the High Dam in 1971, many Nubian villages south of Aswan were flooded in the creation of Lake Nasser.

At Qena a village woman comes to the river for water. Tall unglazed jars have long been in use in Egypt to keep water cool. Despite increasing pollution, the Nile remains the chief source of water.

Figures of Ramesses II are numerous; this one is at his funerary temple, the Ramesseum, in Western Thebes.

Left: *A watchman at the Temple of Seti I in Abydos.*

Used since ancient times to measure the height of the river, this nilometer is on Elephantine Island at Aswan. The higher the water, the better the harvest; former rulers used water level readings to determine tax levies.

Left: *A relief at the Temple of Kom Ombo. Ptolemy VII (145–116 BC) pulls himself through the marsh towards Min, the goddess of fertility. Above and to the right, the king makes offerings to Sobek, the crocodile-headed god, one of the chief deities of the temple. Beneath, the king and his sister-wife, Cleopatra II, are followed by a procession of Nile gods carrying produce from the lands of Egypt.*

The Colossi of Memnon on the west bank at Luxor. Believed by the Greeks to represent the hero Memnon, slain by Achilles at Troy, these two colossi stood at the entrance of the now-destroyed Temple of Amenhotep III. The right-hand statue gave out a musical note with the rising of the sun — the cry of the dead hero to his mother, the goddess of dawn.

*Luxor: in one of Egypt's most spectacular settings, the
Temple of Hatshepsut at Deir el-Bahari rises in
elegant terraces; once gardens and trees grew in front of
it. Behind the cliffs lies the Valley of the Kings.*

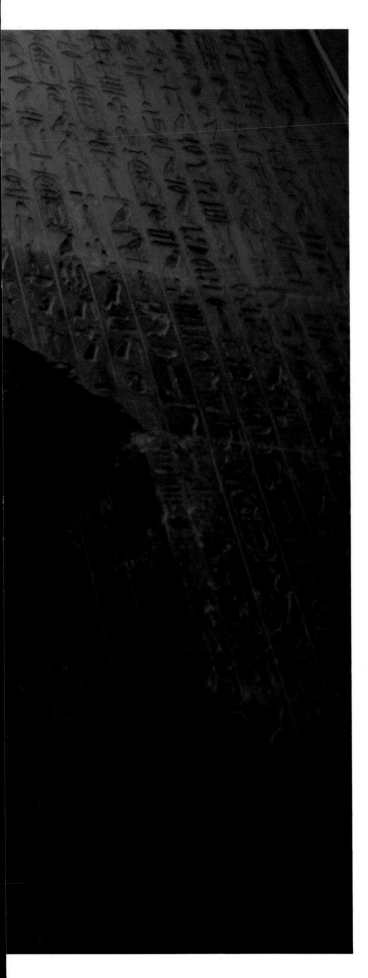

The Sanctuary of the Great Temple at Abu Simbel, which was designed so that on certain days of the year the figures of Amun-Re and the king, Ramesses II, would be lit by the rays of the rising sun.

Left: *Inside the burial chamber of the Pyramid of Unas at Saqqara. Unas was the last king of the Fifth Dynasty. Hieroglyphic texts describe his rebirth and ascent to heaven to join the gods; in one, the 'Cannibal Hymn', the king eats the gods to take on their power.*

The goddess Hathor in a relief at the tomb of Sety I in the Valley of the Kings. Considered as representative and protector of womankind, Hathor is the most important of the Egyptian goddesses. She is also a goddess of beauty, music, precious stones, perfumes and foreign lands. Hathor is often shown wearing a cow's horns and a sun disc, for, according to a creation legend, she emerged from the waters of chaos and gave birth to a sun disc.

Remains of a mummified foetus buried with Amunhirkhopshef at his tomb in the Valley of the Queens.

Left: *Maximizing land for cultivation means that living space is limited, and often families share a roof with their livestock. This is a crowded outskirt of Cairo.*

A desert cemetery near El Minya.

With more than 12 million inhabitants, Cairo is the largest city in Africa. Seen here from the desert of Giza in the west, the contrast of styles of architecture is striking.

170

The mosque is also a place to rest and talk with friends after prayers.

Left: *Worshipping at the shrine of a saint in a Cairo mosque.*

Following page: *The Great Pyramid at Giza was built for Cheops (ca 2589–2566 BC) of the Fourth Dynasty and has since ancient times been acknowledged as one of the wonders of the world. Lacking its smooth outer casing blocks, pillaged to build medieval Cairo, this man-made mountain consists of massive blocks of stone, the largest weighing 15 tons. The exact method of its construction, however, remains uncertain.*

*Although the Pyramid of Chephren (ca 2258–
2532 BC) at Giza is smaller than the Great Pyramid,
it stands on a higher hill and so dominates its larger
neighbour. The upper part is still covered with smooth
limestone casing blocks, once glistening white.*

Excitement is high during a televised soccer game at a street-side coffee shop near Sohag.

175

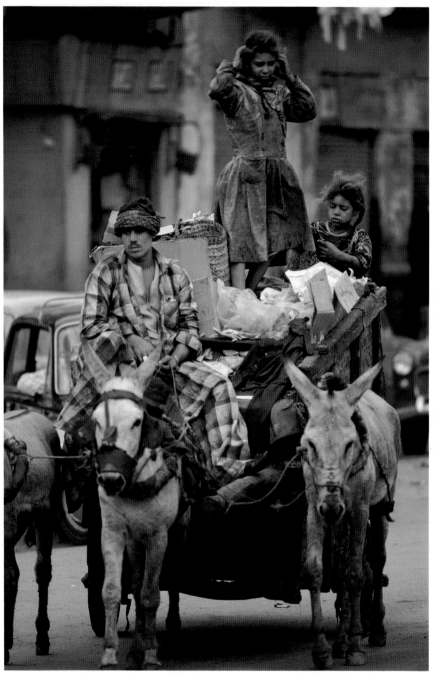

This Coptic family collects garbage for a living. Later it will be sorted and recycled for other uses.

Left: *While the muezzin calls through a loudspeaker, this girl minds the donkey cart while her brother collects garbage in the market.*

*Many participate in public worship on Friday noon
(the Muslim 'Sabbath'), filling the street when there is
no more room in the mosque. At the designated hour
buses will stop to let passengers descend for worship.*

A statue of Ramesses II in Ramesses Square, in front of Cairo's main railway station. It once stood in a temple dedicated to him — now destroyed — at the city of Memphis, outside Cairo.

Because of crowded living conditions socializing and relaxing is often done on the street. Above: smoking a waterpipe at an outdoor café; Right: *typical sights of street life downtown.*

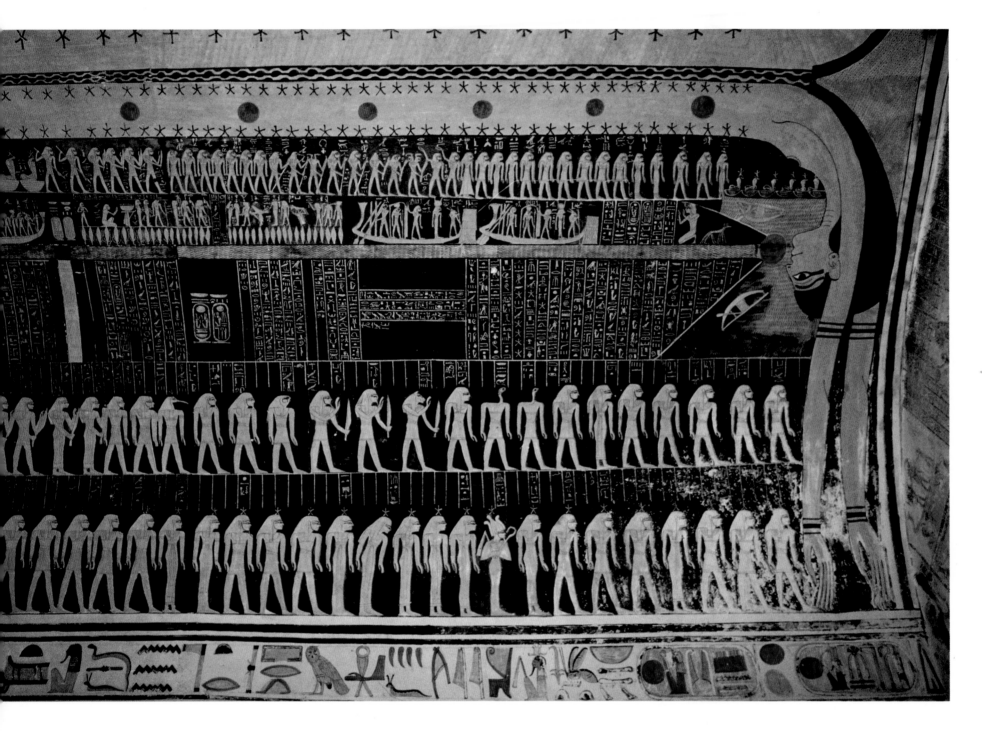

One half of the ceiling of the burial chamber of
Ramesses VI's tomb (ca 1141–1133 BC) in the
Valley of the Kings. The goddess Nut stretches the full
length of the ceiling. She is the sky, covered with stars,
and her feet and fingers touch the earth. In the
morning she gives birth to the sun (left side) which
travels through her marking the hours of the day until
she swallows it in the evening (right side). Then it
travels in her body through the 12 hours of the night,
shown on the other half of the ceiling.

Left: *This pyramid at Meidum — thought to have been built by King Huny (ca 2637– 2613 BC) — partially collapsed 10–15 centuries later, leaving a strange, block-like interior.*

Below: *A corner of the Temple of Karnak, Luxor.*

Here under sail in the twilight, the felucca is an eternal image of life on the Nile.

Kazuyoshi Nomachi was born in Kochi Prefecture on the island of Shikoku in Japan in 1946. He became a freelance photographer in 1971, having studied with the photographic master Takashi Kijima. He is the author of seven books of photographs and essays, including *Sahara*, published in six languages. Kazuyoshi Nomachi has had numerous exhibitions and received many awards, including 'The Best New Photographers' Award' from the Photographic Society of Japan in 1979. His stories have been published in *Life*, *National Geographic* and *Stern*, among others.

Geoffrey Moorhouse is a fellow of the Royal Society of Literature and the Royal Geographic Society. His books on travel, history and cricket have been translated into many languages. *To the Frontier* won the 1984 Thomas Cook Award, and his latest book is *Imperial City*.